My Love For You

written by

Candace Megan

illustrated by

Alexander Lee

My sweet, beautiful child,
there's something you should know.
My love is always with you,
wherever you may go.

It's greater
than a mountain,

more vast
than any sea.

It's stronger than a hurricane,

and taller than a tree.

It's shiny like the
stars above,

and brighter than the sun.

You are oh so
very loved,
my sweet, sweet
little one...

It's tastier
than ice cream,

more delish than any treat.

It's
crunchier
than pickles,

and more ticklish than feet.

My love is far more powerful than the mighty lion's roar.

It's something more incredible than anything felt before.

It's more fun than a carnival,

and stickier than goo.

Until the very end of time,
my love is stuck to you.

THE END

(just kidding, there is no end)

To my three beautiful children:

This book was written for you. Hailey, Kayla, and Ashton, you will forever be my always.

www.ingramcontent.com/pod-product-compliance
Lightning Source LLC
LaVergne TN
LVHW071134160826
845679LV00005B/1284

* 9 7 9 8 4 5 8 2 8 8 9 7 2 *